Part of the Universe

David Flynn

ISBN: 978-81-8253-901-3

First Edition: 2022
Rs. 200/-

Cyberwit.net
HIG 45 Kaushambi Kunj, Kalindipuram
Allahabad - 211011 (U.P.) India
http://www.cyberwit.net
Tel: +(91) 9415091004
E-mail: info@cyberwit.net

Printed at Repro India Limited.

A river that flows beyond where we will ever go.
A sky that spreads beyond where our eyesight can see.
Ultraviolet, uhf, infrared faces looking at us that we can't see.
I have lived decades and have learned one thing:
I know nothing.
I am just a body moving through dark matter.
I am just a brain attached to neurons, light receptors, sound wave antennae on either side of my skull.
I believe. I am wrong.
Still, I love life with so many chances,
and what if those chances come to nothing,
More chances breeze by.
You are wrong.
This is the most difficult thing between us.
"Thing", my favorite word,
because it so vague.
Relax.
Accept.
Me.
And we will be fine.
Read this poem knowing it is wrong.
And we will be fine.
A way, not the true way, not the most effective way, but
a way,
is in these words.
Words, poem, file, page:
We live in so many pieces of cardboard.

So I am going to keep writing.
My goal is 30 pages, a chapbook.
A sample.

A chunk.
Read.
We will both be the better for it.
Somehow.
Don't expect wisdom.
Don't expect insight.
Don't expect truth.
Expect a human
like you are human
but not exactly.

A human is not a logical biological or psychological system.
A human is random.
This poem will be random.
Truth.

1.
Friday sucks.
Not the end of anything.
Not the end of paper work.
Not the end of money woes.
Not the end of reaching into air.
End of a week?
Depends on your belief system.
Saturday's left.
Sunday's left,
Though your church might say Sunday starts the week.
Mine,
well,
that ends when I was a teenager.
Monday starts the week for some.
The end of work?
Not even a pause

because work stays in my brain.
Friday
Fry Day.
French or okra?
Steak or
sweet potato?
So many possibilities
None of which are absolute.
Only French
for example.

This is miniscule, these Friday thoughts.
Today, then, I will be germ size.
Galaxy tomorrow?
You've got to be kidding.
Too many question marks so far.
My questions have no answers.
Such is.
All questions.

2.
I don't believe in necessity.
Randomness seems more realistic.
I don't believe in logic.
I do believe in coffee, cats and clouds,
c's.
Alliteration.
So this morning I woke to rain.
Pitter patter—who says?
Bang bang moist moist flow flow.
The trees are happy, I think.
It's winter. Maybe they're asleep.
We don't know anything about tree thoughts.

Look at those stupid red pants, said an oak
to another oak.
The maple laughs.
Yeah, that human idiot wore a purple shirt yesterday.
I like my leaves much better.
But your leaves are red in the fall.
And yours are yellow.
O.K. O.K. I guess red pants aren't that bad.
Humans, though, they don't even wave in the breeze.

We just don't know.
So this morning I sit drinking coffee, of course,
Thinking about, say,
random here,
whatever comes to mind,
Guitars.
I know three chords, G, D, and C.
Maybe a few others I don't know by letter.
Back in elementary school I had a plastic guitar with a wind-up
knob.
Then in high school a used guitar with a, literally, sun on the back.
Sunburst for real.
I played "Froggy Went A-Courtin'".
Now there's a human logical creation, music.
Organized sound.
Like language, like this poem.
G, D, C. Sonnet, couplet, sestina.
When I talk I talk system too,
not just English,
But when to talk, who to talk to, and when to stop.
"Excuse, Mr. Gangbanger, do you have change for this hundred
dollar bill?"
Nope.

We make a million decisions every day,
which makes life a skill,
not a logical structure.
I'll take that chocolate covered donut with the sprinkles, thank you. Make that two.
Logical?
Don't bet on it,
which would be illogical too.
$10 on that motorcyclist doing a wheelie down the interstate at 90 mph.
Bet he lives the next ten minutes.

What I'm saying is,
to bring this sort-of together,
life is a skill not a list nor a structure,
not even a maze.
We live randomly.
Think you would end up doing what you do where you do it, etc.
if you had a plan at birth
and followed that plan day by day
until now?
Be honest now.
But we aren't honest.
We live in fictions,
like logic.
Or belief.
Or addiction.

End of thoughts; end of today's poem.
Not because these ideas are fully discussed.
But because I am tired.
Later.
Save.

3.
So when I started this poem I didn't expect to write a bit every day.
But that, so far, is how it has been. Is.
Today. Actually I wrote these three lines yesterday, but
from 'Actually' on today.
You see, life is lot more complicated than a Contents page.

So what is the purpose of life, he didn't ask.
I didn't ask.
You didn't ask,
maybe.
One purpose, like a waffle iron.
One purpose, like a traffic light.
One purpose, like a TV.
Except a TV has a billion billion program types:
Catch up on the news,
watch a quilt making show for tips.

Catch up on sports.
So are we,
Father mother worker driver shopper prayer subscriber traveler plus plus plus plus.
Multitudinousness.

The truth.
About?
How to make a good omlette.
The origin of sea weed.
The reason so much wealth is in the hands of the top 1 percent.
Multitudedinousness.

The future.
God.
The soul.
Poetry.
Thought.
DNA.
Multitudinousness.

Skill unites and so we can get out of bed, walk across the room, dress, pour the coffee, start the car,
drive to work, say hello to the supervisor, focus on the form.
Multitudinousness,
But also overview.

Bringing together, filtering, holistic holes, talent, stupidity.
Another damn list.
And together, holistic calibration.
Yeah, a dying child in a cage is bad.
Yeah.

Today I am not in any mood for insight because insight is not in sight.
Get it.
Skills like believing in God, but having no idea what or who God is.
Like believing in love, but having no way to love the whole world.
Like believing in belief, but enjoying the anti, the lists, the new.

That's it for today,
Not because I am finished
or because this was in depth,
but because I am physically tired.
More later.

Less.
Now.
Next year.

Have a great day, as the clerk at the drug store said yesterday.
Great?
I will be satisfied if the Earth doesn't explode.
If I don't die in a ball of fire.
If you don't knock on my door holding an automatic rifle.

Lists of threes.
Sign.
One more part of me.
There are many,
as there are many
parts of you,
parts of snails,
parts of nebulae.
Parts.
What a lovely word.
One.
What a lovely word.

4.
New day.

Chunks.
That's the world.
More like a gravel driveway
than paved.
Whew.
Almost went to clicheland there.
The road of life.

At least driveway means me.
Chunks.
Back on that thought.
A new day.
Lots of parts continue;
some parts are new;
some parts are today only.
So the skill is in living not in analyzing.
Analyze, soak those thoughts into the rest, do, think, plan, regret,
lots of parts.
For example,
and we do need something specific, concrete, physical here to
relate
this abstract wandering to.
Say a car.
The car turns on, the radio starts, the heater gushes,
and I'm off to the grocery store.
The car, however, is composed of thousands of parts,
knobs, pistons, tires, a battery, headlights, etc., etc.
The skill of the car, however, is that it moves where I want it to
move.
I don't think about digital displays.
I think about groceries.
The car thinks about moving too,
and not about its radiator,
U
unless, of course, the radiator leaks.
So the car is composed of thousands of parts,
but is also a whole.
As the universe is composed of nano parts, more,
but is also 'the universe.'
What I have to face now is that a lot of our beliefs, our skills,
are wrong, but we still live until we die.

A Hindu nationalist believes, Rama and Sita and all that,
and thinks Christians are fools.
Vice versa, and a thousand other incorrects as well.
But the Hindu nationalist lives until he dies.
He walks across the room and out the door,
which he could not do if he worried about every step,
the nature of steps,
the relationship of a step to love,
and an infinity of other parts.

Here he goes again.
Parts.
Skills.
Overview.
Of course, I, the reader, can walk out the room.
I've been walking out of the room since I was born,
maybe pushed first, then crawl, then stagger, then walk.

Thank you.
You just proved my point,
Although I would reject the word 'prove'.
You've just agreed with me.
But that's not necessary.
Believe something else.
See if I care.
We both can walk out of rooms.
I can type.
You can read.

Onward.

5.
New day, new chunk.
I got up at 3 a.m. to help my wife pack,
so I don't have a brain left.
The world is a fog,
a milk,
a field of razor blades.
I dread tomorrow.
O.K., bad day,
but it's a day too.
Increments these days.
Modules.
A train of day cars.
And by day I mean night too.
Night day night.
Unit.
I stumbled through this one,
mumbled to everyone,
acted brain dead,
and here I am,
still cool in my own opinion.
Negative day, but
maybe positive day manana.
Maybe.
One, one, one, one, one.
On and on.
Until gasping hurting headache death.
And don't get me started on death.
I'm going to pour a glass of wine,
chardonnay,
then sleep.
We all sleep.
You, reader, sleep.

Tomorrow.
Let it be whipped cream.

6.
New day, #6.
New hour.
New minute.
New second.
So many divisions we ourselves proclaim.
Happy New Second.
Not so much.
No fireworks.
No hats.
No champagne.
2020.
I like that though.
We humans like round numbers: 10, 100, 1000.
When I lived in San Francisco back in the 1970s
the newspaper used to number the suicides jumping from the Golden Gate Bridge
until, that is, they saw that when the number got close to a round one,
#100 of the year say, several people would kill themselves the next day
to be that magic 100.
They stop running the suicide figures.
Quantum entanglement,
do something here and it affects something there even though there is a billion miles away
Aand has no apparent physical connection.
Ghosts.
Do you, reader, believe in ghosts?
I'm not sure.

Spooky things have happened to me,
Like a candle that had been dead for almost a year blazing after a friend died,
blazing so much it woke up my wife and myself in the middle of the night,
and blazing for several nights afterward.
My friend's spirit?
Coincidence?
Coincidence seems more supernatural than the friend spending time with me after death.
I have mentioned several times before that I KNOW nothing.
I believe a lot.
I have a lot of skills,
like walking across the room.
And I continue whether knowing or not.
until I don't continue: death,
Whatever that is.
I, in my old age, have gotten O.K. with that.
Better than knowing 1-78 are the way things are,
when they aren't.
Life is a skill,
like playing the guitar.
A guitar player doesn't think
O.K. I'll put this finger on this string and this finger on that string and another finger on this third string,
and I'll use the pick to strum and make a noise,
then change and put this finger on this other string, etc., etc.
Chords.
The guitar player learns the chords, plays them, knows what rhythm, etc., plus a lot more,
like what emotion, like singing at the same time, like, everything for the song.
Skill.

Like writing.
The writer doesn't think O.K. capital first word, and I'll choose this word, then I need a verb, then I need this feeling, then I need . . .
The Writer writes.
Skill.
Living, as I said, is a skill.
A deep skill.
There are, of course, good guitar players, bad guitar players, professional guitar players, amateur guitar players, etc., etc.
Good writers, bad writers.
Good people, bad people.

So another day.
Another poem.
Chunks.
I like chunks.
You, reader, should like chunks too.

7.
Tired chunks today.
Got up at 4 a.m.
Dark out the windows.

About halfway through this poem.
And.
Always and.

Rain is another part, and it is raining.
Cold, dark rain.
Cats are hiding in their holes.
Birds curl up inside trees.
Deer?

They're big so I don't know where they hide from the wet sky.
Maybe they just stand there, dripping, thinking about dryness, and smiling.
Don't know.
We are such romantics.
Bambi in water,
waiting for the grass to grow.

I of course am indoors under a roof between walls.
The temperature here is always 72 degrees.
This is as much a fictional world as Tolkien.
Food waits in the refrigerator,
40 degrees or freezing.
Another fictional world,
a Wonderland of packaged food,
milk in a jug, cheese in slices inside plastic, pimento cheese with jalapeno slices in a tub.
And TV.
It's off now, a black horizontal hole,
But on it's a news anchor sitting behind a desk in, where?,
Atlanta, actors pretending to be a family,
Detectives on the trail of a rapist.
The fantasy world is a cable surf away, ten seconds per channel, ten seconds per world:
Laughter, sadness, atrocity, dance, food on a stove, someone traveling in China,
a doctor treating immense men and women.
Happiness, sadness, shock, indifference.
It's a wonder we can really feel anymore.

Two hours until I pour the wine and relax toward sleep.
Forever.
Wasting time.

It flows even without us,
And flows even with us.
Grab it, stop it, tackle it.
Dumbass idea.
I am eight years from the average life expectancy.

Good night, moon; good night, transmission; good night, smoke detector.

8.
What this poem lacks so far is stories.
We humans like stories, separate, chunk-like stories,
With humans we can project ourselves into,
either limited and real, like To Kill a Mockingbird,
or unlimited and unreal, like How the Grinch Stole Christmas.
So Christmas.

One Christmas maybe twenty years ago I attended midnight mass at the Cathedral
toward downtown Nashville.
I got out about, say, 1 a.m., and for some reason I hadn't eaten dinner.
I was hungry.
So what restaurant is open at 1 a.m. on Christmas morning?
Waffle House of course.
I drove to a Waffle House through a bit of snow and a bit of ice.
Nashville was white, one of the very very few White Christmases in the city's history.
I sat in my booth, the waitress brought me the menu, I studied it.
Then I noticed that a lot of the other diners had gone to the windows on the far side,
pointing to something outside.
I did too, curious.

There, walking down the frosty sidewalk, was Elvis Presley,
White tunic, black hair, a guitar strapped across his back.
We watched Elvis walk until he turned at the corner and we lost sight of him.
And a feeling of such spirituality filled that Waffle House
that it was Christmas to the max.
I went back to my booth, ordered my food, and smiled.
I have no explanation for this.
Why would some man dressed like Elvis, complete with a black wig,
be walking in the frosty night in an area without bars, without stages,
with only interstate ramps and closed drug stores?
I will never have an explanation.
Still, that Waffle House was transformed,
Christmas.

This is the story that popped into my mind, sitting at the computer on this new day, a Friday.
It isn't the Christmas season.
Make the most of it.
Randomness is a strength, can be a joy, often is reality.
This event was random, my putting it into this poem is random, your reading it is random.
An expected treasure.
Or maybe you think Elvis is hokey?
Then it's a funny story.
Make the most of this random piece of glass.
Celebrate random pieces of glass.
They are all we have.

More stories later. We need narrative to believe bits stick together, make a row, make a day. Or a night.

9.
I wake without a plan.
That's another chunk I need right now, a plan, a direction, a GPS.
Stuck.
But then so many, reader, are stuck too.
The condo, the marriage, the job, the car, the clothes.
I'm in a hole, a silo, a ditch.
We are in danger of cliché-land here.
But then that just means it applies to most people.
Free as a bird;
No they're not. They at work up there, looking for mice to eat, defending territory, making nests.
Free would mean money, rooms of money, millions at least,
And I am struggling for one thousand.
Even with money I probably wouldn't be free,
The condo, the marriage, the car although a new better one with a heated steering wheel.
I'm not asking for much.
So I want to describe another few hours of my life like the Elvis one,
when something larger than the smallness I wake to happened, and a mystical feeling of largeidity—heah, I can make up words if I want to—occurred.

My wife and I were in Kathmandu.
Yeah, I know, just happened to be in Kathmandu, were you?
Nah.
But we were in Kathmandu.
I had proposed on the terrace of the Lake Palace Hotel in Udaipur, India, sunset on the water,
Birds nesting nearby.
"Will I!" she said.
So we were set.

Kathmandu was in the monsoon season. Many an adventure there.
But we spent a couple of days up in the mountains at Nagarkat, which was basically a ridge facing the Himalayan Mountains.
Or at least we were told they were there.
Rain and clouds obscured everything, even the valley that stretched below the terrace of our room.
A sign showed the range of mountains including one little pip off to the right, Mt. Everest.
But we could see nothing.
"Don't be disappointed," the one man in the lobby / café told us.
"A British woman stayed here a week
and she didn't see anything."
So I set the alarm clock for before sunrise the next day, our last chance, and went to sleep.
When I woke up I got dressed, and opened our room door with a sad feeling of doom.
But there, spread out from right to left, were the Himalayas.
The air was crystal clear.
Mt. Everest, Annapurna, detail of rock and peak, and the green valley below.
I woke my wife so excited I could hardly stand still.
We made coffee with the coffee maker, and sat on the terrace.
Pink rays of the rising sun spread from behind the snow-white summits.
The day began with the Himalaya Mountains rising before us.
A couple of hours later the clouds returned, and we saw nothing more,
but in those few hours, especially the first moments,
something huge, and spiritual, and a gift spread before us.

Elvis, the Himalayas, the connection for me is that they came without explanations.

I could list other such unexplained moments, though nothing like a ghost with teeth dripping blood.
Small.
But glimpses at freedom.
I am not free.
You are not free.
We are part of numerous systems.
And we are wrong.
Safe?
Nah.
Happy?
Marginally.
Saintly?
Only by our own definitions, which we sin against constantly, even.

So another day.
I don't expect resurrection.
I don't expect dancing on air.
But I smile when I think of the holes in the stone wall:
Elvis, the Himilayas, the other mysteries.

10.
A trip to my home town today, 120 miles west.
The cemetery.
My father and mother with the same headstone,
my grandfather and grandmother with the same headstone.
Below a magnolia tree.
And across the cemetery another group of headstones,
my Great-Aunt Charlotte and my Great-Uncle Ross,
Great-Aunt Maggie, Clara.

I can't be buried here.
I can't be buried.
Death isn't far off, and I still don't know how to remain.
Ashes in an urn?
Ashes scattered for the rain to take them away to the ocean.
Me in a box eight foot underground.
Bones, somehow?

Am I my thoughts?
Then I will be zero after death.
Do I have a soul?
I have always hoped so,
but detectors that can detect particles so small they not only can't be seen by human eyes,
but that require millions and millions of dollars to pay for the machines that can see them
can't detect one soul.

I was shocked years ago when I realized the Catholic Church teaches that resurrection
means resurrection of the body.
This body will return after death?
With the painful knee?
With the big raspy mole on my waist?

I am just along for the ride.
You are just along for the ride.
Something will happen
ids a questionable statement.
Death/rebirth.
Incarnation re.
Hell.
All those dirty thoughts.

Heaven.
I am too stupid to be pure.
Purgatory.
I am waiting during life; why not waiting after life.

Too many questions.
Damn.
That's all we are capable of doing, creating trillions of questions.
Answers are beyond us.
Live in questions then.
Be satisfied with that.

Can my mother, father, grandfather, grandmother, great-aunt, great-uncle know I am standing there
by the headstones?
I don't know. I don't know anything.
Where are they?
Questions, questions, questions.
What's left in the box after forty years?
Bones, and if bones are they still thinking there?
I don't know. I swear, I don't know.
You, with your screaming beliefs, don't know either.
The suicide-bomber pulling the chord and blooding a hundred people he doesn't know
doesn't know either, though he thinks he's just going to someplace else,
someplace better.

I return to the graveyard every few months despite the long interstate ride.
in case.

11.
I am a snowglobe of thought floating through the air.

Even I think that's a terrible image.
Snowglobes don't float in air for one thing.
And they're cute, snowing on pandas, on the Taj Mahal, on New York City.

So a bad start to today's poem.
A depressing week ahead, blah blah blah.
Little sleep, blah blah blah.
Same old same old work, blah blah blah.
Living for the weekend.
Like living for the Bentley.

So.
What's with you, reader?
Reading this long, long poem on the screen of your iPad, phone, Kindle.
We're all just Save and Delete these days.
Some Copy and Paste too.
Whatcha wearing?
I can't see.

I am wearing my AC/DC pajamas, black and white.
I have Batman pajamas too, Bang! Pow! Whap!
But am essentially a serious man.

Today I can't be profound,
But skim.
Humans can't concentrate on the unknown for long or we develop headaches
instead of insights.

I don't believe in insights anyway, as you know by now.
A day of trivial silly lost directionless shallow hopeless chirpy seems likely.
No nouns today.

I see page 30 up ahead, but a few days to go before my form ends.
This, I admit, is a wasted one, but
that's part of the 75,900 days I've approximately had so far to figure things out.
Haven't.
Won't.
Can't.
Don't ignore silly days.
They are real too,
with deep days
real and not to be ignored.

Bye.
Tomorrow is another day.
What a dumb-ass statement,
I've got to stop this.
Adios.

12.
I shouldn't write at night.
By then my feelings are at my feet.
I don't believe I can do anything, much less write.
But
it is night now.

Usually I wake up, drink coffee,
and new and fresh and propelled by caffeine

I write.
I couldn't today.
Up at 5 a.m.
Work.
Lunch.
Nap.
Cereal.
Here.

My body is a dark sky
Without stars.
My brain is a TV set turned off.
My heart pumps and doesn't feel.
Headache.
Eyeache.
The wish to be in ten different places in ten different directions, and not sitting in front of this screen.
Here.

That's all I'm going to write this day.
I wish you the best.
I really do.
I'm.

The question tomorrow is: should I number this part 13.
Unlucky, you know.
Don't believe in superstitions, but because I lived in Japan I shudder at 4.
My birthday is 4-4, April 4, the worst possible.
I smile at 8.
American, I suffer triskaidekaphobia, fear of Friday the 13th,
Three for the trinity and nine for a trinity of trinities.
Good.
Read the numerology of that 50 years ago and still smile at 3 and

9.

Elevators used to have the 12th floor then the 14th floor.
Maybe tomorrow will be chunk #14.

14.
I feel better this morning.
A night's sleep.
Can't say the future looks any more interesting,
But I have this day made.

Let's see what pops into my mind.
Giraffes.
Cool, but I don't have any experience with giraffes
other than in a zoo.
Once I visited the zoo in Nikolaiv, Ukraine.
A student accompanied me, to practice her English.
I taught for two weeks there, Female American Writers, Contemporary American Writers.
We came to a white peacock.
A beautiful bird tucked in.
He or she looked at me, and walked forward a little.
He or she turned and let fan her enormous white tail.
One of the most beautiful sights I have ever seen.
He or she looked over her shoulder at me.
I took a picture and waved.
The student laughed.
The opposite in a zoo on Bali.
Huge tigers roamed beyond the fence.
One passed me, taking pictures with my iPhone.
He, had to be, stopped and growled.
The sound was the growl of the universe.
He looked at me with hatred, snarled, then walked on.

Same zoo I rode an elephant.
Bump bump bump.
The elephant needed shock absorbers.
A young man sat around its neck, the driver.
I hung on the platform thingee.
After it was over a woman asked if I wanted to feed the elephant.
Sure. $30 for a basket of corn cobs, squash, beans.
The elephant was brought to the other side of a fence.
I took the cob from the basket and he opened his mouth.
Then squash.
Then beans.
I have never seen a look of such ecstasy on any creature, human or not,
as on the elephant.
He brushed my cheek with his trunk.
He, I swear, smiled at me.
More food.
He didn't want to leave.
When the driver led him away, I swear he looked back in sorrow.

We don't know a thing about what goes on in the minds of any animal, or bug, or tree, or plant.
I've said that before.
I'll say it again.

I don't even know what goes on in my mind.
Sure, I hear the thoughts.
But what?
Consciousness is an issue in psychology, I've read.
Is there such a thing or is it an illusion?
And I ask, is there consciousness after death?
If not, we are nothing.

I'm not schizophrenic, although a hacker claimed I was.
Still, if it wasn't for my one conscious self I wouldn't exist.
Exist is a concept of my brain,
one I've learned through reading, school, who knows where else.
I write therefore I exist.
At least with you, reader.
You exist because you read me, in my mind anyway.
If my brain was cut in half
would I exist?
Probably not.

Thoughts that lead nowhere.
That, as I have said again and again, is life.

15.
A bad day.
Wife sick.
No sleep.
Got mad at my first class that came in late and late and late,
and wouldn't shut up shouting and not paying attention.
Student got up and left.
I feel washed out.

Afternoon class was good though.
Such it is, bad and good, good and bad.
Mediocre.
No discernible pattern.
Wife's better.
Class is O.K., except for the one student. I'll talk to him later, reassure.

So this is page 30.
My form.

My sonnet.
My sestina.
30 pages arbitrary,
But I will cut off as scheduled.
Next time maybe 50 pages.
Maybe 1.
Chunks. Different days next time. Different chunks.
I won't bring them together.
That would be my brain making mistakes.
The skill of living means I wake up again, another day, more chunks, sleep.
Then another.
Heading toward death.
Then?
I have no idea.

I will keep writing until the bottom of this page.
Will cut lines if necessary.
Will add lines if necessary.
To fill out the form.

Tomorrow

16.
Could age be a reason for this type of poem, randomness as a virtue.
I am now 71 and have 3 years to go until the average life expectancy of 74.
I have no faith left in thought. The end. Of this poem. On to the next.

17.
Oh crap.

I changed the font size from 11 to 12.
Now it is 32 pages.
I have to cut 2.

Shall I compare thee to a summer's day.
Thou art more lovely and more temperate
Shakespeare—Times New Roman—12 point

Shall I compare thee to a summer's day.
Thou art more lovely and more temperate.
Shakespeare—Times New Roman—36 point.

Such are forms.

18.
Well hell.
I am 3 pages over.
Won't destroy the universe.
The form certainly influenced what I wrote,
but I don't feel like cutting 3 pages.
It's a good thing.
I have written more than the form dictates.
More.
More.
More.
Good for me.
You want two kids.
You have three.
Do you kill the one?
You want $10,000,

and get $20,000.
Do you throw the extra $10,000 into the wind?
Nah.
Draft #2.
I discovered milk and honey.

1.
A new poem, a new page length.4
4 pages, 4 days.

Yesterday was a lousy one.
Today more sleep and life seems better, less splashy, flatter, more in gear.
Not really, but it feels that way.

Wife is better.
Her heart race was 105 beats per minute; now 78.
The heart beats billions of times during our lives; what a creation.
Greeks debates where the human emotions were located: brain, heart or knee.
We give hearts for Valentines; the heart is a symbol of love.
Can the kidney be a symbol for cohesion.
Can the pinal glands be a symbol for transubstantiation.
No questin marks because those aren't questions.
I heart my city.
Lub dub lub dub lub dub.

So nothing solid to start this poem.
4 pages because I want to try something shorter.
See where it goes.
Having given up belief in unity of thought,
Adhering to chunks,
As I said before,
Let us see, reader, what falls from the sky next time.

2.
A day with nothing to do, cloudy, cold.
Doing nothing is a waste, but clears the brain.
Only so many days can be filled with work, with problems, with tension
Before the body collapses,
The thoughts turn to death,
The end of this crap.

I have often thought of suicide, but haven't.
Once I wrote a novel about suicide, instead of.
That was last year in fact.
A friend, one of my oldest, committed suicide a couple of years ago.
Shotgun to the heart, pull the trigger, splattered, dead.
I had just talked with him a few days before.
We had planned to attend a journalism awards banquet a few days after.
He won: Best Humor Column.
Nobody seemed to have been warned or suspect.
Pull the trigger. Bang. The end.

I haven't because life goes up and down.
I don't want the down to destroy the up,
Though the up isn't all that up.
Besides, who knows what awaits in the afterlife.
Maybe nothing.
Maybe something worse.

So I just let the day bump along,
Pray,

Wait for the next day
Or the next.

Until, of course, I have that cancer.
A car swerves into my lane on the interstate.
A teenager pulls a gun in a grocery parking lot, and shoots me in the head.
A heart attack.
A bomb.

Who knows?
Death is going to happen.
It is going to happen to you, reader.
We can ignore death or make it part of life.
Our sense of death is what makes us improve our lives.
If we thought we were eternal we would lie around all day,
Napping, eating, not thinking.
Death leads to computers, airplanes, poems, prayers, marriages, families, stock exchanges, football leagues, existentialism, punctuation, frozen gyoza, songs, movies, air conditioning systems, and
Almost everything.

3.
I'm almost on the last page.
Four pages just isn't enough.
But the form I set was 4 and I am going to stick to 4.

Worries.
That fills my brain today.
Two big ones in particular,
But a ware house of others too.
Can't think about eternity.
Can't think about the nature of God.

Can't think about cohesion and touching and passing it on.
The worries like bears stand in front of my eyes
And block the world.
The world jumps around, I see.
Is full of colors and shapes.
But brown hair bears roar and bear claws close up.
Can't shoo them away.
Can't kill them.
Can't make friend with them.
So today
Bears.

4.
Last page.
So soon.

These poems have become journal entries.
I haven't missed a day since 30=page poem began.
Tired, headachy, busy, Super Bowl, work.
These lines keep coming, including the day,
And including my thoughts as I sit in this chair this day.
The same.
The End. But it is never the end. Just a sentence in a long book bound by birth and death.
Imagine a pile of 7 billion such books. That's the world. That's this poem.

666 words?
Can't do that.
The mark of the Devil. Nero's name in numerology.
Add more.
I'm not superstitious.
Just neat.

1.
I changed the font to Times New Roman, and the size from 11 to 12 lines.
The poems became more than my forms of 30, 4, and 1 so far.
And if I double space the poems, of course, they go way beyond the page form.
Suppose I were to take Shakespeare's sonnets, and change the font size.
The lines would be different.
So my form in these poems is page number, and the font given by Word.
Single spaced because that's what Word began with.
I should have noticed.
I didn't.
So sue me.

2.

3.
Too tired to write poetry yesterday.
I was on an all-day panel interviewing applicants for a Japanese exchange program.
I know.
Not typical.
But I wanted to give those strangers the other.
Japan.
Out of the ditch and into the forest.
I was in the teaching program thirty years ago, and
It gave me the world.
Good applicants all. Those curious. Those empty. Those searching.
The world.

1.

Even a philosophy book, say Neitzche, is a journal.
His thought those years.
The ideas are not eternal.
Nothing human is eternal,
Except that we were here on this one planet
For 1, 2, 3 years.
The rest, all, takes place without us.
That's not sad.
It is real.
Even that idea is melting ice.

2.
4 hours of sleep last night.
I know; I was wearing my Fitbit.

Hacker posting loves messages to women who are friends
From me
On facebook.
Changed the background photo on my iPhone to a man
He accuses my wife of having a crush on.
Ah, current life.
Internet and hackers,
Humiliation and destruction.
This is only a glimpse at cyber hell.

So I want to think about something else.
Food.
Ice cream.
Egg nog ice cream.

Double chocolate ice cream.
Molasses and peanut butter ice cream.
I make these in the summer.
This is the winter.
A dusting to an inch of snow forecast for tonight.

I know these are specifics and details,
But they are what life, what God, what purpose is made of.
Shingles.
Twigs.
Feathers on the asphalt.
That is really all I know.
Putting them into a structure, well,
That's where humans fail.
I've said this before in these poems:
Ever theory we have of life, of metaphysics, of death
Are likely incorrect.
So don't kill somebody because he's in the wrong political party.
Don't kill somebody because he believes in a God with a different name.
Don't kill somebody period.
Live and die.
That's our story.
Live and Die,
My next novel, my last novel, your next novel, your last novel.

Today, after 4 hours of sleep, maybe r.e.m., maybe not r.e.m., this is the best I can do.
I am on the literal level of my brain.
Stop.
Sleep 8 hours, according to Fitbit,
Then tomorrow maybe I will write better.
Let this be a sample of mediocrity.
For now.

3.
Whatever I write is what I write.
That's magnificent.
That's the day.
Whatever I do is what I do.
There are continuities, of course:
My personality, my thought patterns, my attitudes.
These make the poem one,
Just as,
The day makes a life one.

Here I feel the urge to relate this abstract thought to an object.
Seems some readers can't relate to abstract thoughts.
Not you, current reader.
You're smarter than that,
More skilled at vagueness.
But for those who need thing thing thing to understand thought thought thought
Let's say a 2 X 4 wood board.
Blonde, cut from a tree trunk by a metal toothed saw blade,
Noisy, emerging flat on all sides, wide, thin, conforming to human systems in that
It is two inches by 4 inches and so so inches long.
Inches being a mathematical construct created by humans and not found in the world
Without humans, nature say.
Continuity in that the cells of the wood, created by a tree, now deceased, are separate but
Create a unity, the board.
Poor tree, minding its own business, growing, photosynethsizing, communicating by chemicals
With the other trees in the forest,
And some human comes along with a power saw and cuts it off

at the base.
Process, international companies involved in the manufacture of the saw, the gasoline that powers it,
The clothes of the lumberjack, etc., etc.
My, is this complicated.
Everything is complicated.
That glass of water you just got from the faucet involves pipe manufacturers, glass manufacturers,
Treaties between nations, factory construction, etc., etc.
I should name this whole this Etc., Etc. But won't.
Anyway, back to the board.
So abstract thought is like the board while daily detail is like the wood cells,
Which themselves are composed of chemicals and such.

Didn't help, did it?

I plan to give my wife a Valentine with a heart on it in a week.
The heart is a symbol of love.
Why?
It's a gushy red bloody yuk.
The dove is a symbol of peace.
Flap flap. Poop.

Today's poem didn't go as I had thought it would.
Of course.
Nothing does.
Not Naturalism, not Democracy, not theories of the consciousness.
And it doesn't matter.
It went as it went.
Follow your dreams, the cliché says.
But also follow your thoughts, follow your emotions, follow your

chance, follow your plans that
Aren't true, follow your truths, changing, wrong, inept, follow
your days, follow your years, follow
Your death.

4.
I woke up this morning feeling dead.
Tossing and turn all night.
Money terrors, life nightmares.
One final dream
About murder,
And I woke but not completely.
I walk around now with a head that thinks about failure.
I don't smile.
I ache.

This might be what the afterlife is like at first,
Half awake,
In a watery dream.
Aware that I am dead,
But having no way of consciously reacting to that.
Who could?
Good-by everybody I knew,
Wife,
Daughter,
Cats,
Colleagues.
I have never been completely alone,
Alone with no hope of ever seeing another human.
But I will be then.
Still in my brain,
Fading,
Going.

I've been thinking a lot about death lately.
In my 70s,
Closer than before.
And I have come to no conclusion.
Death is an adventure,
I thought.
Then delete.
Death is a meeting with angels and God.
I hope.
Death is meeting old friends, my parents,
Except I am nervous about my parents.
They, we, were not ideal.
Sure.
I'd see them, live down the street from them, or better
Across heaven town.
Hell town.
Purgatory town.
I don't know what will happen.
Will there be pimento cheese after death?
Will there be good books?
Will there be interesting conversations with other dead people?
Will I talk to Thomas Jefferson?
Richard Byrd?

I hope I wake up this afternoon.
I did write this while dead.
Later, days, I will read it and be surprised.

5.
One of two money terror days coming up.
A meeting to determine if there is a special assessment for roof repairs in our Association.
Could be $10,000 we owe.

Tax day is next Saturday.
I am ruled by money.
You are ruled by money.
Despite hard hard work everything I have earned will earn may go into assessment and tax.
Then what?
You have a regular job, regular wage, swell. Live a regular life.
Without it creditors screaming at you, summons to court, how do I pay $20 for gas.

Money controls poetry, controls morality, control democracy.
In fact, democracy is dead.
You would need millions to so much as run for mayor.
Pay for it yourself or sell yourself to a rich person(s) who will.

I would like to find some apartment, casita, rented house somewhere,
New Mexico, New York, Buenos Aires, Captetown, Osaka
Where I can leave the world.
No internet.
No news.
No movies, no television, no stores.
But I cannot.
If I would be a hermit I would have to buy a cave.
Maybe $200,000.
Food delivered by Grubhub, Uber Eats, whatever,
Paid by credit card.
Money from where?
I would be feral
At least for awhile,
But the economy of the woods means constant dodging of fangs and claws
Wanting to eat me

Or me killing raccoons, opposums, wild turkeys.
But wild turkeys would turn on me in a group of feathers, beaks and claws.
And what would I do all day?
Think?
No, I am stuck with being alive
Until I'm not.
I could, of course, commit suicide this mornig,
But that doesn't seem like an improvement.
Insurance would pay my debts.
But.
But what?
I don't know what awaits
If anything.
Something good and bad for something that is nothing.
Maybe.

This whole poem I have faced the fact that I don't know.
You don't know.
They don't know.
So bilge.
Guess I will go downstairs and eat lunch,
Shredded wheat with banana slices today I'd say.
I can't know the immense;
Welcome then the tiny.
Breath, heart beat, hair growth continue
Whether I want them to or not.

6.
Bhuddists say live in the present.
If I live in the past I am suffering dementia
Where the memory dies from the present back in time.
If I live in the future, well,

I am optimistic.
If the present is horrible,
Make the most of the horror,
I suppose.
If the present is heavenly,
Smile all day long.

Most of us live in the past, the present and the future.
Isn't that better? More?
Born in Tennessee textile mill factory town,
High school hood,
Off to college in Missouri,
Off to college in Colorado,
Reporter for a Memphis newspaper,
Trip to South America,
Camping in a taent
Down the Pan American Highway.
Year in Memphis writing a novel.
Editing a construction magazine in Minneapolis.
Unemployed in San Francisco.
Married in Nashville,
Working in Personnel for the State,
Then teaching at an Historically Black University.
Off to college in Boston.
Off to college in Nebraska.
Six part-time jobs in Nashville.
Divorce.
Year teaching in Japan.
Temporary teaching job at an Historically Black University.
Teaching job in Hawaii.
Writing residency in Ireland.
Writing residency in Israel during the First Intifaddah.
Teaching job at a Japanese uNiversity branch in Hawaii.

Teaching job at a community college near Nashville.
Writing residencies, five in Taos, New Mexico.
Fulbright to The Former Yugoslav Republic of Macedonia during the insurgency.
Propose to wife #2 at a maharajah's marble palace in Udaipur, India
"Will I!"
Fulbright to Nikolayiv, Ukraine.
Marriage #2.
Retirement.
Fulbright to Indonesia.
Teaching part time, English and Asian Studies, at Belmont University.
Teaching full-time, English, at an Historically Black University.
Sitting at this computer,
Listing the past.
Present.
Sitting at this computer.

Future.
Driving to school to teach a class.
Valentine's Day this Friday,
Flowers, cake pops, a bracelet, socks with our wedding date, dinner at a Spanish restaurant.
Maybe a trip to Portland, OR, this summer.
Maybe. The Future. Maybe.

Death.
Nothing.
Nothing.
Nothing.
Nothing.
Nothing.

Nothing.
Nothing.
Nothing.
Nothing.

7.

Late at night.
Miserable day.
I don't want to whine
Again,
But really.
Can't I inhabit the groove.
Can't I make tapioca pudding
Without the damn toilet breaking down.
Let the valley of nails appear.
I'll tiptoe through it.
Ouch ouch ouch.
And maybe,
Just maybe,
There's a valley of champagne beyond.
Swimming through the bubbles,
Sipping the lake.

I know that's really bad, but that's today.
I don't want to be awake.
I've asid that before during these lava flow periods.
But I am.
Up and down up and down wall.
That's life.

I hope you are having a good day.
That's what every clerk in every store in the city says.

To be more exact
Have a great day.
Great days are rare.
Bad days are frequent.
O.K. days are frequent.
Good days are not the usual.
But if every day was good
I'd be stupid.

Let me finish this with a blessing
From an ordinary man without powers.
May you survive,
And have the occasional good news.
May you not sink.
May you look back on your life so far, and think
Could have been worse.
Maybe the toilet will fix itself.
I'm an optimist
With pessimistic eyebrows.

Sleep without a tree falling on your bedroom.

8.

This poem has become a journal,
Recording the thought and feelins
When I sit at the computer
Each day.
It hasn't recorded the actions of that day.
Currently I am teaching fur sections of a freshman composition course
At Tennessee State University.
That dominates the actions of my life during the week.

Wake up early, stday tired, teach about the five-paragraph outline, the summary conclusion,
Sit in my gray office four hours, teaching the same class to another room of students,
The five paragraph outline, the summary conclusion,
Comma splices, change of person.
Drive on the interstate, survive the cars, the trucks,
Condo, feed the cats, feed myself, nap.
Dinner, write the days part of the poem.
I know this is boring.
So are your lives:
Wake up early, shave, dress, eat, drive the interstate to the office, check the files, and so on.
Or some such.
That is how we live, survival.
I am not putting that down.
We live with necessity.
I am not sure there is a real alternative.
Bank robber?
The arrest rate for robbing banks is huge, almost certain.
Drug dealer?
Check with the gangs and live another few days.
Beggar?
Too much competition on the downtown streets.
I am tempted to move to Buenos Aires,
And might if my wife left me.
Cheap, so my social security check might pay my expenses.
Not here in America, not even close.
Interesting, the old district,
Tango, Astor Piazzolla, gauchos Ushaia, the wine country, the Andes, Indian country in the north.
Write, eat, die.
Social security is as close to being a hermit as I have available.

And a small TIAA pension, $500 a month.
No car payment, no insurance payment, no utilities.
Peace?
I doubt it.
Humans are incapable of peace.
I often read the opinion that the past was a simpler time.
No way.
Rotting teeth and pain.
The Civil War.
Life expectancies in the 30s.
And that's the 1800s.
Imagine being poor small farm, peasant type, in say Romania, in say the 800s.
Wake up early, work all day with the dirt and the pigs and the cow, if lucky,
Die of the plague.
Human life now is simple as it has ever been, and it isn't simple.

So, reader,
If you ar reading this when day is done,
Sitting on the sofa with a glass of wine before sleep,
Know that this is our lives.
No one likely will read this,
Or few if I am lucky with publishers,
Which I have never been,
Whine whine whine on the sofa,
But if you are reading this in repose,
Repose away.
It won't last.
We need clearings
Or life is all forest and brush.
You know what I mean?

9.

Little sleep last night, turning from left to right, tension, panic, worry like a bullet
Stream.
Tonight a heavy meal, roast beef, carrots, mac and cheese.
Red wine, a mix.
So I am a cloud
That knows only that it's a cloud.
Nothing about Carthage.
No love hugs.
I'm a cloud for goodness sake.

So here's a poem,
The first thing that pushes into my mind:

I'm a jar.
A jar doesn't go far.
I sit on the shelf.
No sense of self.
I'm full of flour
White, self-rising flour.
Been months since I was lifted,
After I was sifted
In a factory
Where I became me.
Some day I will bake
And the man or woman will make
A biscuit to eat.
I have no feet.

O.K., I'll stop.
Tomorrow I will reach for God.
Tonight I will just stop.

My apologies to you, reader.
I have wasted two minutes of your life.
But I have wasted three minutes of mine.
A life is all a waste.
But that's fine.
That's us, trivial, frustrated, glimpsing a golden field from a passing bus window.
Let's at least dance in the aisle.
For us.
Reader.

Bad day for writing poems.
See you tomorrow.
Maybe.
Always maybe.
That would be good on my tombstone: Maybe.
Except I want to be cremated.
That would be good on my urn: Maybe.
Actually I want a shock of my hair
In a shadow box
With a picture of me.
Perhaps the one at the Great Wall.
Perhaps the one wit the Love sign on the store wall.
I want the shadow box to be on a shelf in my wife's living room.
Too painful though.
Maybes more than one box,
More than one shsock of hair.
My ashes in the urn
In a cabinet.

Useless.
No way to hang on.
Just throw my body in a cave

To decompose.
A year later: bones.
There is no way to make death any sweeter.

Tomorrow.
I think I can make it to tomorrow.

10.
It's tomorrow.
I think I can make it to the next tomorrow.

11.
There are so many part to think about,
Sex, insects, sectarian violence, sectional sofa,
But why?
Self-reliance isn't possible.
What we call self-reliance is just the individual making good in the economic system.
A job, cleaning his own apartment or paying a cleaning service, the individual doing his own income taxes,
buying his own groceries.
Even in the past self-reliance was a gun
Or a farm.
So now I am one in 7 billion, soon to be 10 billion if I'm still alive.
Even a president doesn't stand out much,
And that's among humans.
One in 10 trillion for let's say ants.
May be more.
I have counted and nobody else has either.
For viruses, vira?, it's who knows the term, can'timagineillions.
I O.K. with that.
What is is what is is what is to forever which doesn't exist.
I love you forever,

Or until a teenager pulls into my lane on the interstate and smashes into my car,
Which almost happened yesterday.
Almost: yet another title of my autobiography and of everybody's autobiography.
I almost met you, but you
Decided to eat at the café next door to the café where I ate,
So we never saw each other
Much less looked deeply into each other's eyes
And said,
"I love you to the edge of the universe."
Or rather ths universe,
Because physicists say there may be other universes.
How many people have I never met?
Almost everybody.

So a day where, again, I just walk and see where it leads me.
Should I grab life by the collar and shake it?
Shouldn't I aim at the moon, and take the first steps there?
I'd stay on this rug, doing steps.
Life doesn't have a collar; it has heart beats, breaths, sneezes.
Have to go.
Got an appointment.
Taxes.
Crap.

12.

It's Sunday.
I am bored with writing these poems.
You are probably bored with reading these poems.
I am writing.

Bored is one of the most useless words;
A plain of a thousand miles we have to walk.
Fill the plain with thoughts.
Fill the plain with projects.
Fill the plain with the rodents, the insects, the plants that grow on this level ground.
Bored means I am a failure.
Entertain me.
Staff, make me a grilled cheese sandwich.
Life, where are the jewels, the cars, the parties?
I should never be bored.
You should never be bored.
Death, if we think, will be really really really boring.

So of the quintillion times infinity times infinity part of the world
What should I write about this morning.
Bees.
I thought of bees as I sat on the sofa drinking strong coffee,
In my pajamas.
I thnk of bees now.
We can't eat without bees,
Pollination and the plants we chew on.
Bees are striped.
Bees have stingers.
Bee society worships a female, the queen.
Bees die after sex. Sexual suicide.
Drones in tight shirts.
Bees roam the planet, looking for flowers.
Pistils.
Bees buzz.
Bees be.
I am glad I'm not a bee though.
Bees don't have computers.

Bees don't have cell phones.
Bees don't have poems.
But, I'll bet, they do have a lot we don't have,
Like flight.
Honey factory.
Oh mighty queen, we worship thee,
Nectar of the universe,
Source of all beelets.
We live for thee.
Hive home matriarch.
Males don't even have stingers.
Female government.
Female society.
Beemale.

I can always entertain myself.
Bored's butt.
Something will happen today.
Borsch.
I'll make borsch.

You, wake up.
You have hours, like velvet bags, to fill.
Fill them with honey.

13.
Yesterdays amateur ramblings about the bee
Covered maybe ten bits out of say an infinity minus 57 of
What could be said about the bee.
Honey bee or bumble bee?
Or.
That is true of everything: say celery.
An infinity minus 118.

Dust.
An infinity minus 77.
Hair.
An infinity minus 46.
We just don't have the time to understand anything.
We can learn a tiny bit,
And use that,
But as far as understanding of the universe, life, truth, God, that sort of thing,
We can only glimpse the heat waves.

I have said before, good enough.
Riches fly all around us.
Enjoy, use those.
Rule the world?
What a joke.
Even Caesar, even Attila, even the president
Rules so little.
O.K. president, tell the locust not to invade Kenya.
Uh huh.
O.K. emperor, tell the sun to wink.
Uh huh.
O.K. world's richest man,
Yeah man unfortunately,
Buy my heart beat.
Just try it, man.
World's richest woman,
Buy all the penguins.
Just try it, woman.

Borscht.
I made that last night.
My hand turned red from the shredded beats.

Ribs.
My wife asked, can you eat those?
She had never eaten ribs.
Imagine.
Cabbage, white beans, carrots, the aforesaid beets, ham, beef, pork ribs.
Borscht was a bowl of red warmth on a cold winter's day.

I know.
Shut up, David.
Borscht yesterday, leftover borscht today.
So it goes.
90 percent of my life is leftovers,
Leftover job,
Leftover car,
Leftover TV
So little of life is new when you reach 71 as I have,
Or 30 for that matter.
Anything really new happen in your life?
A new wife or husband doesn't count?
Leftovers.
A new country doesn't count.
One more.
A new religion doesn't count.
Been there all along.

You know, I really do love life.

14.
Why is there air?
It's a joke, something a kid would ask a parent and the parent be bumfuzzled.
But really, why is there air?

Why is there anything?
Why is gneiss?
Why is there tapioca?
Why is there hockey?
Why is a troubling question.
We always assume there is a purpose.
To whom? To who? To what?
Why is there air?
Some would say it's a natural chemical reaction,
But that's materialism.
Some would say it's a gift from God so we can breathe,
But that's metaphysics and assumes
A circular purpose: we breathe air, or air breathe we.
Why do we have to breathe?
We could have been born with a different system
That didn't need oxygen.
Too many questions.
It's like life is all questions.
Well, maybe it is.

My daughter once asked my ex-wife if "It's." is a sentence.
She had learned at school that "It is." Is a sentence.
Of course "it's." is a sentence.
Just not a usual one.
It exists.
It's.
He's.
She's.
We're.
They're.

15.

The soul.
Why hasn't there been a huge scientific effort to prove the soul exists and to explore its nature?
The moon, that's O.K. Shining up there bald and pocked.
But if there is no soul, then half of our beliefs are gone.
If there is a soul, then half are proven.
Celebration. Let the crowds cheer.

I am not sure what scientists could do with the soul.
A soul-o-meter.
A vast underground soul accelerator.
A satellite aimed at the Earth.
They deal in the material, although
Quantum entanglement, subatomic physics, and parallel universes
Come close to the spiritual.
Maybe the spiritual is measurable, like voltage.
I don't know, but angels, devils, the Trinity, Rama, the flow, the dharma
All need investigation
From outside belief.

When I was about twelve, sleeping in my upstairs bed,
The Virgin Mary came to my bedside and touched me on the cheek.
You will say I am crazy,
Or just a kid with a wild imagination,
Or a Catholic school subject—all those God is good; God is great recitations.
But I tell you,
The Virgin March not only appeared by my bed
When I was conscious,

But, and here is the vastness,
Touched me on the cheek.
I felt her fingers pressing into my skin.
I did.
Sixty years later I am prepared to take a lie detector test, anything, to prove this happened.
Although, cynical reader, you will say it was a false memory, an obsession, a boy.
But I tell you, the Virgin Mary appeared at my bedside and touched me on the cheek.

Emerson says children are the smartest of us.
They have the most direct communication with God.
As we grow older we are filled with human detritus, like education, like experience with society, like life.
And that comes between us and God.

So why isn't there a vast governmental effort to find God?
We care about the smallest of things, the flow of electrons in titanium say,
But not about the biggest.

17.

Inspire or uninspire.
Clear or cloudy brain.
These lines started as poems,
And by now are poetic journal entries.
My thoughts this day.
A slice o life.
Because if I write this next month,
The thoughts will be different.
So it is.

So is life.
Not organized.
No thesis.
No syllogisms.
Just bam bam bam.
And overall
Skills.
That's where we get into trouble.
Overviews.
I feel confident in saying this is how I feel now about this,
This is what I think now about that.
The meaning of our existence, however,
Moves below my feet
Like alligators.
Like.
Associations.
I don't care if they are good or bad.
That's the best I can do this day.

18.

Free to be anything.
Free to be a slave.
Free to be a philosopher.
Free to be a football player.
Free to be a retired teacher.
Free to be Xenophon.
Free to be Marcus Garvey.
Free to be free.

The mind certainly can be anything to a spot.
I can get on stage and pretend to be Caesar.
I can use computer graphics and be a unicorn.

Not anything like the original of course,
Not the same fingernails,
Not the same food likes and dislikes,
Not the same sex thoughts.
A plastic bag of the heavy weight of reality.

And so are our thoughts.
I can think about the universe, and be
A body sitting in a chair on the second floor of this condo in Nashville, Tennessee.
And not the universe or anything like it.

That's just the problem.
We think and the thought isn't the thing.
It's a thought.
Duh.
Small electric charge running along neurons in this swishy cauliflower we call the brain:
Akira Kurosawa!
Technique and not comprehension.

Once again I will write about the first thing that pops into my mind.
Today that's
Phlogiston.
Phlogiston was a substance released during combustion.
1800s.
Only it doesn't exist.
We call the process oxidation, which is different.
So for awhile scientists tried to measure the phlogiston released during, say, a fire.
Oops.
The Earth is flat, 8,000 years old, and the center of the universe.

Still people lived, loved, suffered, exalted, the life stuff
Even while wrong.
Wrong about the most basic bits the world we drive through.
I just searched on "age of the Earth."
The answer: 4.53 billion years.
That's wrong too.
Maybe we should rename the Earth Wrong.

And I'm not sure the Earth is the center of everything.
Remember Music of the Spheres?
This was the idea that the stars exist on clear spheres and the circulate.
Where they rub together they create sounds we can't hear,
The music of the spheres.
Actually, instead of sound it was more like a harmony.
Most people believed that until about 1600.
Still they lived, loved, etc.

Say 300 years from now
What will humans believe?
Relativity? Hah. That's stupid.
A consciousness? Hah. That's stupid.
Osmosis? Hah hah hah.

But what I don't want you to believe is that I am cynical.
I enjoy the misses, the beliefs, the mistakes.
There is a richness to a world where human stumble about,
Guessing this, grabbing at air and thinking they hold a stick.
Suppose we did know everything.
How awful that life would be.
No surprises.
No yearnings.
No curiosity.

Humans can't know for sure, anything.
Let's rejoice in that fog.
It's wet, it's white and churning,
It contains vampire, and queens on horseback,
Kings wearing crowns.
My dear wife, my dear daughter, my dear granddaught.

I need a theory to walk across this room and down the stairs to lunch.
That's O.K.
I don't have to think about moving my legs.
Skill moves them for me.
Skill runs the economy.
Skill runs the churches.
Skill runs love.
Each different.
Each not united.
Each good enough.

19.

Today is a good day to go crazy.
Lemon taste.
Misty rain.
The time I drove from Tennessee to Los Angeles. Make that times.
Candy cigarettes.
How to pronounce falafel.
Black birds building a nest on a white marble maharajah's palace in a lake in Udaipur, India.

I look forward to being demented.
True, I will miss the present,

But in a world of my own
I will say hello to dead friends,
redo a mistake I made in 1974,
erase erase erase back to my birth,
which I don't remember,
but neither did my mother, under drugs.
I can wave to people I knew as I pass backward.

If I am incapable of knowing the truth about life, the universe, God,
Then being insane doesn't sound too bad
Unless I am physically insane, of course.
Mentally insane doesn't sound that much different from the minds of everyone
Now.
We have a billion borders, like a wooden box, or a page, or a plate,
Borders like don't kill that woman who slobbers in the airplane seat next to you,
don't yell at the man blocking the grocery aisle examining a can of peas for minutes,
don't leave your family even though they cost too much.
Commandments?
Ten is just the start.

Borders are needed to keep 7-10 billion people walking down the sidewalk
Without bumping into each other.
Concealed weapons indeed.

If automatic rifles are legal why can't citizens carry nuclear weapons?
Just a side thought.

So I can't be totally crazy today,
Just a dot of crazy on the endless white plain of life.
Well, not endless, but it seems endless.
I seriously cannot imagine death,
And I can imagine a flying rabbit delivering pizza.
I think I can make it through this day, however.
Breathing, beating, seeing, moving
I'll be O.K.

Hope you are O.K. too.
Delete.
I can't do anything about you except pile some new ideas, beliefs, personality bits
On your already immense pile.
Let's walk through the valley of the shadow of death together though, O.K.?
Valley?
Death is all around this condo, all over the street in front, all over this skyscrapered,
Tall-and-skinny apartmented, parked, restauranted city.
It's a sunny day, so let's walk through the valley of the sunshine of death
Together.
See you later,
When we both will be different.

I don't get that period at the end of the sentence finale to today's writing.
I feel awkward.
I feel disunited.
Maybe I am crazy today.

20.
Watered the plants.
Indoors they can't water themselves.
Outdoors in fact they can't water themselves.
Plants can't walk, can't swim, can't fly.
Stuck at the spot where they are born.
I have been around the world twice.
36 countries so far.
The land is pretty much the same,
But the people are different,
Different clothes,
Different houses,
Different religions.
Well, not so different clothes and houses now because of TV, the internet, a general Earth culture,
Business and America.

In Indonesia they have hip hop, the blues.
A restaurant featured a live country band playing "Rocky Top" and "Take Me Home Country Roads."
Older Javanese culture: shadow puppets, a ballet with Rama and Sita, and a 500-year-old sword I bought
For protection.
That's there, somewhere, but in the streets are thousands of motorbikes, Kentucky Fried Chicken,
Canned foods in the groceries.

Plants have a culture too,
Leaves and stems and chemicals.
They talk to other plants with those chemicals.
They panic if too dry too long.

Rocks have a life,
Slowly eroding into gravel.

Earthquakes, tsunamis, volcanoes, floods, sure,
But usually breezes, below freezing temperatures, and the sun.
These are actions.
These are what move everthing, us, through lives.
My brain is still liquid so I write.
I slept, dressed, drank coffee, climb the stairs, and sat typing at this computer.
You?
Another liquid day.

I would like to be a vine n the next life, if not a rich human.
A long, green vine with plenty of leaves.
Yeah. So much better than a slug
Or a pond.

Frog spit.
Worst food I ever ate, Taipei.
A bowl full of green scum.
Real pond scum or a cook's creation? I don't know.
On the menu it said "Frog Spit."

I took a plane to Taipei.
I moved.
No plants, trees, ferns, vines or grasses occupied the other plane seats.
No cows, no raccoons, no buzzards, no spiragyra either.
Ain't humans something?
We move.
We wear down.
We age.

We die.
The ultimate airplane.
To where?
You think they'd tell us.

Mazda, a car I once had.
Mazda, a Zoroastian god.
Starbucks emblem features a Scythian goddess. If it was full length we'd see her tail.
We don't worship these, but we drive them, we drink them.
Buddha ash tray.
The cross coat rack.

So I am not saying one thing today.
I am saying several things.
That's all I really want to, can do.
Have a great day, as the clerk in the store says.
Me, I'd settle for an interesting day.

21.
22.
I think yesterday's ramblings were not saved.
Oh well.
Lost a part of me.
There are many parts.
Many parts to you, reader, as well.

I want to float.
Walking is so awkward.
Step step step.
Bend knee.
Leg one leg two leg one leg two.
We don't glide

We harumphhh
Across a plaza.
And running.
The same as walking except
Pushier.
I do like to walk around cities,
Especially New York.
The detail is lost in a cab.
Walking I see the bricks,
I see the homeless,
I see the jazz clubs.
So far I've been lucky.
Haven't been shot, stabbed, or robbed.

Once in Rome I was walking near the Coliseum on a back street.
A knot of teenagers were walking toward me,
Clearly aimed at me.
I moved to the middle of the street,
And stopped,
Staring at them.
They had been tense;
Now they broke up and passed around me
Smiling, hissing, shaking their heads.
I think I avoided something.
Nobody else was around.

Such is life among humans.
We are all just a wall from being murdered,
A block from being robbed.
Leave the condo, and
I feel exposed, in danger,
Among gang members, the ragers, the desperate,
The professionals.

It used to be—
Oh Lord, here he is again with this old fart nostalgia—
Used to be that you knew the person who kills you.
Now, it could be a 14-year-old waiting in the grocery parking lot.
Death by strangers.
Sounds like war.

Like I said, I want to float today.
But my mind keeps going to dangers,
A bump on my stomach,
Scabs on my legs,
A ragged back of a tooth that wasn't ragged a week ago.
Buddhism says live for the present.
In the present I worry about the past,
I worry about the future.
Cut that out.
Concentrate on this keyboard.
Don't think about the rain outside,
The bills,
The scowl of the supervisor.
Fingers.
Letters.
Numbers.
Punctuation marks.
These words that appear on the white 'sheet' of Word.
No, I just can't do it.
I am pastpresentfuture all at once.
I need to take a class in meditation,
Zazen maybe,
Nothingness training,
To float.
Today I will bump along the ground like all the other days.
Floating makes me smile.

I still want it, like I want ten million dollars to smooth out life,
Like I want more sleep,
Like I want no job
Except writing.

It is 2020.
I have my doubts I will be alive in 2030.
Maybe.
Probably not.
1948-202?
That would be on my tombstone,
Which I don't think I am going to have.
Fertilizer for a tree would be more useful.

Glide well, reader.
We are all just dear compost.
Don't frown.
That's better than just customers.

23.
Micro mini nano.
Mega bazillion forever.
One.
There we are.
Now I can write something.

Blah day.
Average day.
The usual.
Boring. Well no.
Exciting. Not even close.
I'm lined up.
I'm on the narrow path.

I'm standard.
Smiled at by a lot today.
No threat.
Reliable.
Friendly in a general way.
Quick.
Gone.
Not remembered.

If I had clucked like a chicken, got down on all fours, and scratched the dirt
I'd be remembered.
If I had flapped my arms, squawked, and bitten a passerby,
I'd be remembered.
Instead, I swim through the water and the water heals.
Another like life.
We swim through the water o' life,
And when we are passed
Life heals.

Don't you just hate metaphors.
I am a watermelon,
Rough green and streaked on the outside,
But red juicy and full of seeds on the inside.
Not quite sure about the parallels there,
But that's a metaphor.
A miniphor.
A betaphor.
A whatphor.
Well, why not those too?

Tuesday.
Twosday.

Two minds,
I hate;
I love.
Nah.
I don't feel;
I love.
Nice to meet you.
O-genki de.
Don't catch the flu.

It's night.
Dark descends.
No it doesn't.

24.
9 Hours of sleep last night.
The first time for enough in months.
Does that do something to me?
My dream world,
20 %? 10%.
I would say 100%
We all live in our brains.

Ice cream isn't necessary,
But it is,
Double chocolate, rocky road, egg nog, Heath, vanilla bean.
So good.
One summer I made bacon ice cream.
I can see lettuce ice cream,
Red bean ice cream,
Chocolate pineapple apple ice cream.
If all of life was made from the necessary
We wouldn't smile.

Frivilousity proves we aren't rocks.
I don't really need that shirt with the flames on it.
I don't really need baseball.
I don't really need hip hop.
Come down to it I could probably get down on all fours and eat grass.
But I don't.
Tortilla chips for lunch,
And not filtering krill.

Celebrate.
Living in my brain today
Means I can't take traffic tragically.
I can't be discouraged by my sore knee.
I can't worry about how I am going to pay for 2021.
Threes again.
I think in threes,
The trinity.
9s, a trinity of trinities.
Numerology.
666—Nero the prosecutor of Christian's name.
4 is bad luck in Japan,
Shi means four, shi means death.
8 is the good luck there.
I don't know why.
Fear of Friday the 13th, triskaidekaphobia.
We all could be expressed as numbers,
And as numbers live in computers,
Maybe for centuries.
Then a hacker would steal us,
Demand ransom or we would be deleted.
Save a thousand of yourself
If this happens in our lifetimes.

Live on not only on paper,
That letter you wrote fifty years ago and which
Is now in a plastic bin in a storage shed owned by the friend you wrote to
In college—
But in digits.

So now I have to go.
Job.
Abrupt end.
But if you have been paying attention,
Iffy,
You will know I believe nothing begins and nothing ends.
We live in slices, then segments, then modules, then 1,
But that is our skill uniting an overview
Which is a slice by itself.
Besides, I believe
Is not solid either.

Living in my brain.
Yeah.
Now there's a truth.
What is truth?
7 billion brains,
And the rest of the universe too.
Maybe universes.
We just don't know.

Have a great day.
Or at least
Survive.
Oh hell,
Enjoy the frivolous.

That's what I've been writing about today.
Ice cream,
The sunset,
Playing Solitaire on your cell phone.
Have a frivolous day.
Oh hell,
Have any kind of damn day you have.
I quit.

25.
Disconnected.
The title of my album o' life.
Right now I don't have a thought,
Don't have a brain.
Cloud fog blind bilious you name it.
What a day.
What, a day?

Let's try rhyme.
Italian Renaissance revenge.

I sit in my chair
Breathing the air.
Thinking of you.
We are two.
Can't catch my breath.
Life'll be my death.
Nothing seems set.
I need a net.
Kiss my tired lips.
Sips. Black flips.
Face it, rhyme seems childish.
Ideas seem mildish.

I'm quitting this now.
How now brown cow.

That was a waste.
Good days and bad days for poetry and this is a worse day.
See you in the golden morning,
Rays of gold sun through the dirty window.
To morrow.
I declare this day done.

26.

3 plus pages to go for 50 in this form.
It's not that I will quit thinking after those pages,
Or writing,
But that the sample will be done
For this time.
Even if I had written sonnets,
The sample would be the same,
Just formatted differently,
A different length,
Different expectations,
Different rules from other people.
Write a sonnet:
I accept the rules.
Don't write a sonnet:
I have to make up my own rules or expectations or lengths or something.
Many possibilities.
I have written sonnets before, and sestinas, and haiku, and all such.
But that's not the boundary of poetry.
Apparently it is easy to rhyme in Italian.

Hip hop, rap accepts that and makes English rhyme strong again.
Not chirpy, not cliched, not rule-bound.
I accept rhyme too,
And alliteration, and metaphor, and associations, and Freudian objects, and ear worms,
And everything else my brain uses.
Are there limits?
I am human.
Limits are my life.

Reader, listen up.
Spring is coming.
Traditionally spring represents beginning,
Freshness, buds.
I know better.
You know better.
Our lives will continue, joy, despair, hurt, distraction, achievement, all that.
Spring respresents tornadoes, floods, cold fronts, snakes eating baby birds,
Three months afater the new year.
Let's celebrate spring, but don't get too giddy.

A man stands on the corner of my town displaying a sign saying the Rapture is coming.
He's been there for years, still visible.
But still believes.
I don't agree, but envy him his continuing belief.
He just knows.
I know I don't know.
As long as he doesn't kill those who don't believe in the Rapture
He's O.K.
I am still trying to find a universe to believe in.

27.

So I have solve nothing in this poem,
Or any of a lifetime of poems
And stories
And essays
And journalism
And photographs
And prayers
And university degrees
And work
And marriges
And daughter-granddaughter
And cooking
And eating
And walking
And talking
And everything.
I have lived 71 years so far though,
Made it through the bamboo
The pine woods
The open fields.
I feel hollow.
Live until you don't, I've been telling people.
My wisdom,
Along with: life has its ups and down. You're
In misery today;
In a year you might be happy.
You're broke today;
In a year you might be solvent.
You are loveless today;
In a year you might be breathlessly holding kissing feeling.
Wisdom like ice cubes
Are good only in the freezer.

On the counter they melt.
Damn, I wanted to avoid cheap associations in this poem,
And there is one more limited metaphor.
Add it to the pile on Earth.
Damn. Pile. Another one.

Yet I love life.
Why?
One more page to solve that mystery.
That's the trouble with forms,
Even this formless form.
Focus, maybe maybe not.
Limits. Every time.
I want a poem that includes everything.
That would be the only true one.

28.

Tomorrow I leave for a retreat at a monastery in Kentucky.
I have left out daily events so far,
But that one seems profound.
Thousands of acres of woods to hike in,
A vow of silence,
My Catholic upbringing in robes and chants.
I can't be full Catholic anymore,
But St. Mar's gave me a sense of the spiritual that has not weakened.
I still pray.
Retablos of saints and diety fill my living room wall,
Lydia Garcia, santera.
I don't want this poem to have a sense of climax,
A sense of completeness.
I don't think or feel whole,

Or directed
Or at ease with belief.
I have to live incomplete.
So do you, reader.

Half a page to go for the form,
The 50 pages.
I will have to add lines, take out lines
In other drafts
To keep the form.
Doesn't seem necessary.
If the poems goes into page 51 with a few lines
So what?
Here it is. The last line. 7443 words. For now. This is the universe in pieces.

www.ingramcontent.com/pod-product-compliance
Lightning Source LLC
Chambersburg PA
CBHW022201160726
48282CB00024B/273
* 9 7 8 8 1 8 2 5 3 9 0 1 3 *